Crookedness

Tsvetanka Elenkova

Crookedness

*translated from Bulgarian
by Jonathan Dunne*

Shearsman Books

Second edition
Published in the United Kingdom in 2019 by
Shearsman Books
50 Westons Hill Drive
Emersons Green
BRISTOL
BS16 7DF

Shearsman Books Ltd Registered Office
30–31 St. James Place, Mangotsfield, Bristol BS16 9JB
(this address not for correspondence)

www.shearsman.com

ISBN 978-1-84861-686-8

Crookedness was first published in Bulgarian as *Изкривяване*
(*Izkrivyavane*) by Stigmati Publishing House, Sofia, in 2011
and in this translation in 2013 by Tebot Bach,
Huntington Beach, CA., USA.

*Cover image, The Kiss (after Gustav Klimt), reproduced
by kind permission of the artist, Boyko Kolev.
www.boykokolev-art.com*

CONTENTS

II

For Jonathan

Beauty is symmetry
Plastic surgery advertisement

Wisdom is knowing when to shun perfection
Italian restaurant menu

STRAIT AND SLANT:
TSVETANKA ELENKOVA'S *CROOKEDNESS*

To read any poet who matters is to step into a terrain that's all their own. This terrain may be purely textual, made up of the particular rhythms that form their thought or the formal games they like to play. Or it may be homage paid by the imagination, memory or the poet's eye to places we readers have never visited for ourselves. It may be tonal, a question of mood or atmosphere. It may combine all of these at once and also be yet something more: a transformative visit to another way of conceiving of things, whether abstract or concrete. The best poets take you to a conceptual world you have otherwise never visited, although when you see it for the first time what you feel is recognition. This is the other side of T.S. Eliot's return, in 'Little Gidding', to something seen (as) for the first time: an initiation into the familiar.

For the Anglophone British reader, one of the most obvious recent examples of a poet's terrain must be Seamus Heaney's Mossbawn. The rural Irish way of life is as far removed from the daily, urban experience of most admirers as, say, Pascale Petit's Amazonian rainforest: yet is made equally accessible by how it is written. Brilliant textual terrains many readers have visited in recent years include those of the Canadian Anne Carson or, in the US, Claudia Rankine. (Both writers have highly engaged political agendas, but it's their formal brilliance that actually achieves the feminist, anti-racist work of their poetry.) Working in a different tradition, Tsvetanka Elenkova creates the third kind of poetic world, one that comprises, and offers the reader a way into, a different conceptual universe.

The world according to Tsvetanka Elenkova is both lucid and hieratic. In it, a lover's eye is 'a disc on a chain /with the god of the sun /the window casts on the wall'; but love itself is an 'Altar' on which the lovers are 'lying crosswise'. The poet's own narrative eye keeps shifting viewpoint – and perspective – not for the sake of it but to create depth and meaning: 'The other side of perspective /is dimension'. It's all expressed with economy and the utmost clarity: yet that clarity is deceptive. These poems, too, depend on your point of view: 'Reflection is capture' indeed, and reflection may be not only the untroubled mirror image, but the pause and re-handling of meditation.

Another way to say all this is that Elenkova is a religious mystic; something that her specialist scholarly studies underline. She lives in the world of cars, mobile phones and city parks, and has an imagination stuffed with cultural riches, as a riff on a rose reveals: 'lace/curtains crème brûlée parasol /boat which tugs on its rope /nose by Chagall /eyes of a geisha or lady from the court of Louis XIV /complete with make-up wig beauty-spot / and hairstick'. But she also lives in a poetic world, peopled by a son and a lover, of religious mystery, mortality, love and desire. This mystical verse dives repeatedly into the given, and discovers there a world of symbol and – perhaps above all – movement. It is not Gerard Manley Hopkins's search for 'inscape', but instead an apprehension that from moment to moment forms itself into symbolic codes – and then releases those codes into the material, sensual world.

There is nothing remotely sweet about this:

The other
at the end or beginning
is black
there you enter-exit

is both a shell and the lover with whom, 'you set up camp' between 'the two strokes of 12': that is, in the movement from one (1) to two (2). This kind of active meditation is anti-quietist; it is a violent, ravishing almost, interpolating of self with world, one in which both world and self are to be sacrificed. If that sounds too great a claim for any verse, we could remember that the discomfort with which we try to fit ourselves to these new concepts as we read – that 'leaving the comfort zone' of the familiar – poses us questions about who we are. What kind of readers are we: can we tangle with the mysteries of the world and existence like Elenkova, or would we prefer to retreat to easy-reading anecdote, description, or expression?

Tsvetanka Elenkova doesn't pose us this challenge because she's Bulgarian: in her home literature too, she is simultaneously distinguished and poetically revolutionary. Nor do these poems challenge us because they are fine translations, made by her husband, the poet-translator Jonathan Dunne, from the Bulgarian original. It is Elenkova's consistently searching poetic vision that challenges us. The achievement of her poems is to lend this vision to the reader: so to frame the inexpressible that we too perceive it. Which means that, as we read, we too take part in the mystical transformation of world to revelation.

Fiona Sampson
Carey, May 2019

I

PAIN

When you hold a bottle and hear the wind
through the open throat
when you put a conch to your ear
the echo pain from the emptied body
and when a single slight hiss
as of a punctured bicycle tyre
finally fills the empty space
like a newborn's wail
Take it carefully in your arms
and give it or don't to its mother
but take it carefully
it's so fragile all cartilage
Give it water or leave it on the shelf
by your head

PAIN IS SO CLOSE TO PLEASURE

The question of love and pain
has as much to do with physics
as with the teaching of Lao Tzu
For instance
communicating vessels are not just connected
they feed into each other
And it's very important who is higher
where the flower pot is where the bucket of water
when you're away
So the question of love and pain
has as much to do with Freddie Mercury
as it does with Christianity

POST

The galaxy is a dog's black coat
which opens when combed
you see the skin
or make a parting
then tie two bunches
perfect schoolgirl
the road opens even more
swollen river's dykes
bed dug over centuries
You drop a leaf boat or shell
or just a stick
If it doesn't lodge on a stone or sink
it'll flow out somewhere in the end
dandelion on your balcony
You pluck the black cuticle and know
it's a letter from your lover

HOURGLASS

As under the crown of a broad-leaved tree
which is an upturned conifer
we sit in the shade pick its fruit
or build a tree house
to watch the coming storm
or experience it for ourselves
we experience the death of a friend
relation or our own
and then bottles glass decorations
and then candles lights
of Christmas trees
we never scale

INTELLECTUALS

You send me a photo
of those "honest animals"
living on the border
on dependence
with condescension not humility
like my dog and our infant son
I throw a ball to all morning
to-fro up-down
vying jealously
electricity
not like those meandering sleeves
at airports as well
swollen scattered
in all directions
grey eventually
they will out

CANDLES

That rope
in the stomach the head
between the thighs
all the fire and lymph
which sustains the fire
seeks someone something
to put it out
a noosing of the mouth
around the flame
a licking of fingers
a gentle hissing
next to the earth
after so much
degradation

FISHERS

There is a cobweb
with a wick in the middle
not a spider
but still it blows
in the wind
rebounds
sticks to your legs
in the tall grass
the corners of warped
forests and houses
accidentally blocks your path
on the way to some ancient ruin
almost catches your skirt
tears off a small piece
so sharp
a scratch on your leg
glue between your fingers
not one you'll remove so easily

GLOBE

There where
on the smooth bulging surface
reflection meets reflection
is the pupil
narrow like that of snakes
there is the equator also
the orgasm
the coiling caterpillar anemone
shutter
day and night rains
So don't tell me
above and below
is sky

FRESCO

Start with darkness
like that at the base of a shell
or candle
or the world
scratch away
with tinder in the middle that equation
until you receive an answer
and a grey remainder
which is smaller but constant
and eventually tips things
treacherously
in its favour

CHOICE

There was a bracelet
you bought
but then you hesitated
(or they hesitated for you)
and you changed it
for no more than five minutes
The bracelet had bad teeth –
an excuse to take it back
but you kept it in the end
that wedding dress
those Greek sandals
which aimlessly spontaneously attract
like magnetic backgammon pieces
jumping over their threshold
your brother's blood

THE SNAKE

The rape
of innocence
of sin-ignorance
of just plain ignorance
of the lack of a knowledgeable
instinct

that knot first and last
of the throat
right next to the entrance to the eye
(without passing through)
lots of eyes
stuck in a pincushion

first you try with your fingers
then with your nails
with something thin or thicker
like a pencil for instance
you shove it in
several times to and fro
chains are the hardest
or the tail of St George's horse

until it loosens

then you untie your laces
drop them to the floor
or in your shoes
if you're more diligent
Ready to enter

FATHER AND SON

There where
eyebrow meets eyebrow
the curve fits closely to the forehead
as a fragile stem in the shade
to its shadow
without a curl or knot of hair
in between
its crown
scratched all over by grasses
with the same box form
one to another
sandals laden with sand
coupling of engine and carriage
glove slipping off a sweaty hand
angels
of the day and night
Roman hunting mosaic
you are

RESPONSIBILITY

Though we do not have
an amphibian's flat
bulging pupils
lying on the hard ground
which won't let me sleep
I see you
turning up my eyes
on the amethyst's surface
with your head down
like a Moroccan cup
on a background of falling plaster
or melting snow
narrowing them –
dappled shade you merge with
So I cannot work out
what truth is
your reflection
or sacrifice

STORM

We are all with our head down
the antennas are masts
of upturned ships
a little more and they will sink
in the sea
above them
which thickens
like the Underground
or an overcrowded bus in winter
with steamy windows
and broken shock absorbers
Someone rams into you
you hold onto your bag
frantically wipe your hand
up and down the back of your coat
black
with a seam in the middle
for it not to run
Smell
as of a wet dog
or something boiling which shouldn't
and as you barge past
your scarf caught between so many bodies
zigzag
tightens round your neck
you feel the thunder like your pulse

GABRIEL

Not a drop in a cloud
but a cloud in a drop
three cut sides
of a diamond
little white cloud
when I saw you for the first time
or the man in white
brought you
like that on the Ipomoea's tube
which I photograph photograph
exploding star

DESERT

The kernel is hollow
the longest root
is that
of the Tree of Life
which widens its hole
by rubbing
or plays pinball
with free
and captive balls
the corridor is sometimes narrow
and everything is molecules nesting dolls
left-right
up-down
the spring is most important
where do things end
with the smallest –
a question
of choice

SHELCAN CHURCH

You step on the swollen lens
of its body
thrown onto dry land which makes it
more slippery
You hardly keep your balance
with your hands tied
and then to be safer
they mourn you in a boat
hanging from a cross in the sky
the same a mythological creature
once held on a plate
The balance is simple –
fish bones in a skull
And there above you
milk-filled breasts
cut from crags

DIRECTIONS

Three times a door slamming
revealing rather than revelatory
deep touch on the border
smell on a leash
like that of violets with jasmine
in the pages of a book by Proust
in the long wait between two flights
at a central European airport
a Moldovan stops and asks you
for the second time

THE SEVENTH LAKE

You fly away
horizontally to the earth
(like the dead by the way
who carry on wandering locally
for three days)
not in your reflection
but in that of the slanting slope
turned inward
a far more natural posture
in the whole of creation
even pressing down
The others
though perpendicular (to you) bells
there's always a chance
their shadow
will fall on a rock
make a pointing hand

ABSENCE

When memory becomes expectation
because you know neither tongue nor time
fragmented ongoing expectation
metronome on the piano
like the Strupets Transfiguration
The right hand's praying edge
for cutting now
Or the holes of insects
we know nothing about
but they vanish and reappear
That striving their bread
that dread

SPELL

What is there in common between
our infant son's plastic house
for which he lost the keys
the front door of our apartment
which wouldn't unlock
and that apple stain on my jeans
stage light
before they ripped at the knee
stage curtain
and I threw them out
prior to departure

THIS IS IT

Your body has nothing in common
with the cross
or Leonardo
or the sun god
your hands have something in common
with the restraining gesture of icons
but here it's a question
of an interweaving (of the ankles)
an open
eight
a curve (of the wrists)
which is the base
of a Victorian vase handle
you never hold onto
eternity going on
trembling
graceful

REMINDER

What leaves
a smell
not a memory
giving giving out
carriages
not an engine clothes toys souvenirs
flowers in pots
but cut lasting three days
not just in the sinuses
those fields of roses coming back from Rozino
but that hyacinth that blossomed in the soil
and especially in water is important
not just with the stems down
but fully submerged
when the smell gains weight
becomes flesh
you can almost touch it
No wearing perfume
they said to my son
between two lengths

BLINDING

The line of your shoulder
or that sheet
is the only border
between past and future
your thumb passes over
when hitch-hiking
or learning tenses
not vertically like an emperor
or salt-cellar
or pistol which can also be
a blessing
not the pressing down of walls
before they collapse
but like the four tunnels
we travel through with
our infant son
who doesn't distinguish them from bridges
that telescope of a half-
clenched fist
so you can focus better
he sticks his finger
in

IMAGE NOT MADE BY HAND

He looks not above
but under the cross
stuck in his mouth
on the plane where earth fertilizes
all directions
left and right
two cracks only
and matter is so voluptuous
it pours out
or is squeezed by the borders
those mummies
wrapped inside their bodies
all of this under the dome his seed
flowing hair
girdled circle
of the mandylion
photo board hand
on and on outside
and in him
flat loins
the exit is always down
where there isn't usually
even a door

HOME

The eternal conflict
between nomad and settler
between hearth and ocean
in a game of tug-of-war
in an arm wrestle
someone will eventually win
but how important is
this balance patience
of the hill horizon
running little things
as in the bonds of a molecule
of substances in a hard
liquid
(but not gaseous)
state
those tiny droplets of moisture
which roll down the blade of grass
the edge
you move them with a slight
trembling of the hand
one towards the other
until they fuse
as an angel flutters his wings
you see him on your shoulder
in the rear-view mirror
like a transfer which separates
and you fall silent

GLOBAL WARMING

It hasn't rained for two days
but puddles can still be seen
here and there
which gradually shrink
into tiny coins
Only the dampness is left
even if it's in the air –
that first whiff on the steps of the plane
or his shadow on the cross in the church
of St Mary Salome
This is how our infant son stretches
when he awakes
he stays like that
But the climate is changing
soon it will be hot here
or rain all the time
which is the same

LIGHT DISTORTS

Sharper
than a blade of grass or a sheet
than the edge of a yoghurt pot
but when they cut it
actually it takes a bite
that crescent at the end
of a paper napkin
whole
when you open it out

TRINITY

The blindness of precious things
disappearing
which even memory doesn't help
or constant repetition
or signs before and afterwards
Somewhere among them
and it doesn't matter whether he's the same
or an allegory
whether the first is still in place
whether you will receive the third
or graft in another
he is always lost
alone
in someone's company
or with something in tow
that one in the middle
like the finger of a figure from the choir
in the oldest part of
Santiago Cathedral

RING

Little stones like
the facets of a butterfly's wing
forms of broken glass on
the fronts of village houses
mica
diffract the light blinding it
throw bevelled sun spots
on the white sheet
a monarch astride his horse
the breasts of a wet-nurse
the gold rush
Hubble's latest images
while the hand moves like a spindle
stretching-thickening-disintegrating
with my Bic

ORCHESTRA

Like an organ
which has many pipes
you have to release
the key pedal
once pressed
sometimes whole chords
cycles
her hair on my right
my hair on his left
drums cellos
harrrp
the wilder of the infant pair
the end before the beginning
(this is the Resurrection
not the Return of the Prodigal Son)
the way they wrote
Glagolitic

INTERSECTION

What remains accumulates
and therefore falls away
first prize
or
audience award for
installations –
monk's cross with bead for
girls
salt of the earth
placenta from
Rublev's Trinity

COLLUSION

One click
and you're on the outside
or have lost a finger
children especially
with every folding-unfolding
of wings
I saw on TV
the loading of cartridges
of tubes for gas
buttons even –
the tapping of blind men's sticks
on studded pavements by a crossing –
this absolute unconditional fit
whatever comes before
though often it's euphoria
has nothing in common with
a gentle knock at the door

COLD

Not the weather
but the atmosphere I say
around the head
tied
below or above
like a dove
around the body
it pops
small balloons sucked
into the mouth
a leaf on a hand
telescope
this air distance
this knot a hit
our infant son
throws pebbles into the lake
but when he leans forward
Not closeness
but force I say
and pull him back

DEATH

A sting
after you have lost
your finger

ALTAR

The other side of perspective
is dimension
near-far light-shade
have no meaning
just entering-exiting
your right male eye is a page
or letters' graphic expression
your left – a disc on a chain
with the god of the sun
the window casts on the wall
an open book
The only shadow at its upper end
is yours
the only light above it
your atmosphere
Stay like that you said to me
lying crosswise

IMAGES

Which to choose
The first
the best (or strongest)
which is almost the same
or according to distance where they meet
usually the first or third
or just the one in the middle
You can move the focus
choosing her or something else
(especially in ritual)
or what time has left
(most often a gesture or eye)
Some are interested in the whole picture
or in what they've achieved
From the three jet earrings –
the one that runs

FAN

A quarter and something of the sun
coordinate system or cross
in the centre of which
live four bats
upside down
but with outspread wings
and with the bare eye you can see
the rays of their sounds
centuries
for the sea to smooth them out

SHELLS

There where it swells
is white
no doors
just a peak
or two
stuck like a limpet or newspaper
hat
there after the two strokes of 12
between which you set up camp
the counting restarts
and everything fits
reflections in their entirety
The other
at the end or beginning
is black
there you enter-exit
it breaks
but the hardest thing is getting
from the slope to the steps
where the gap is
except for a boat
in a strip of seaweed on the sand
except for a foot
in a shoal of fish in the shallows

MATTRESSES

Bodies with their moans
stones
the accordion is broken
only the echo is left
and a stuffed creepy-crawly
They could at least put them out in the sun
you said

II

ROSE I

What's inside
water and leaf
on the left
hard and dark
because it's opaque
on the right
light and shade
with a bud on top
like a distaff or nib
a heart in formalin
(Henry IV's perhaps)
yellow contained
cheek to cheek
stone in something

EDELWEISS

You can still talk
even if your lower jaw is
stone and mortar
kerb or ledge
of a window or balcony
above your mouth is down
which glistens glue or tentacle
Even if you cannot shake your head
or hope for wind
you can still talk
It depends on the point of view
You get up and squat
You jump
You stay next to someone who's leaving
so that those on the inside think
it's you
The wind for me is an obstacle

PANSIES

Your eye is reached
through the flowers in the pot
in the hole between two
petals which almost
touch
after it's rained and is sunny
there where you expect to see
soil a sill or even
the block opposite
where you don't expect to see
anything at all
not a bulging eye like Emperor
Constantine's or an iguana's
a drop of paint on the edge
a downward brushstroke
which hardens

PANSY AFTER RAIN

Reflection is capture

PANSY I

You stand on the shore
it's unclear
whether facing or turning
black clouds over your head
and a yellow sea
desert
with one foot deep in the sand
the waves digging it up
ovary
with the other you take a step
any moment to push yourself out
you will drop

PETUNIA

Only when I'm under scrutiny
do I see your eye
the lashes a continuation of the iris
the pores of the lashes
overflowing and rising
rolled-up sleeve
your face purple
and me slightly crouched

ROSE II

The leaf's profile
is the vein's full face
Both in focus
The way

JASMINE I

Four's shadow
is a cross

ROSE III

Because you have many feathers
ribs folds of lace
curtains crème brûlée parasol
boat which tugs on its rope
nose by Chagall
eyes of a geisha or lady from the court of Louis XIV
complete with make-up wig beauty-spot
and hairstick
whichever way they look at you
chiaro-
oscuro
add to that your gardens
frame through a car window
your intensity
which doesn't need contrast
and it's you

JASMINE II

Every drop
starts from your body
and ends with a nipple
shining aura
which is quantum-expressed
to one side is the navel
its cross a base
both in shade
the aura overhanging
yoghurt in a cheesecloth
tied to a tap

blue is many levels
of clarity
white is dark
transparency

a little honey and sprinkled almond
your swarthy face
a leaf arranged
for later

CARNATION

In every flower
is a fish
which strives towards the centre
a whirlpool
quite separately from
the stamens insects pollen
it carries itself alone
in the desert
a transfer
with eye holes and a rocket's tail
falling off
and burning up in the atmosphere

CACTUS

There where it seems
to climb up
it actually goes down
it's so red
it's almost shining
like congealed blood on
or fire behind
glass
it looks round
but up close is square
and somewhere in the middle
is a garden with little white stones
and a hole like those made by palms
between the yachts of a western harbour

IPOMOEA

When you hit the centre
the bulge becomes concave
the spiral a nebula
At such speed
a pilot said
the most important thing is concentration
and I count the steps
from lilac to blue

HYACINTH

It turns out
that giving its hand
as I clean the nettles
it's not a root
but a top
which budded in the soil
so it's fragile
hundred-year bones
sans colour sans smell even
or smelling of a raw egg
I crack in water
fragrant for three days
without changing its colour
it doesn't sprout again

PANSY II

The drop is also rooted in blue
those evergreen plants
hanging in nets
with their soil and
blood vessels like
an Easter lamb's gouged eye
with just a little yellow round the edge
old age and light
three irises –
so you don't pass under a bridge
but jump through a hoop

TULIP

It fills from without
but also from within
boiling milk
wine in a jar
sparkles of champagne
until the petals open
as if along their edges
their final extension
reverse projection
and the withered sweetness overflows
holy oil
grace
wings touching
the lightness we choose by
he says

GRASS

That spot
of a leaf-stuck drop
which has spilled over its borders
like an icon's halo
wave on a rock
Camariñas lace
is someone who stops at words
without seeing herself
and casts back gleams

TSVETANKA ELENKOVA has published six poetry books and two books of essays (one on the Balkans and another on Bulgarian frescos). *Crookedness* is her fourth poetry collection and has also appeared in a French edition, as *Distorsion*. Her previous collection, *The Seventh Gesture*, has appeared in English with Shearsman Books, in French and Serbian. Individual poems have been translated into fifteen languages and have appeared in the magazines *Modern Poetry in Translation, Poem, Poetry Review* and *The Massachusetts Review* among others. She has been a guest at various festivals including Lodève, Struga, Tinos and Vilenica and recently received the prestigious literary award Pencho's Oak for the body of her work. She is the editor of *At the End of the World: Contemporary Poetry from Bulgaria* (Shearsman Books, 2012) and has translated international authors such as Raymond Carver, Rosalía de Castro, Bogomil Gjuzel, Manuel Rivas, Fiona Sampson and the Bhakti poets in *Speaking of Siva* into her native Bulgarian. She is a doctoral student in theology at Sofia University, where she is writing a thesis on mysticism in the poetry of Gregory of Nazianzus.

JONATHAN DUNNE holds a degree in Classics from Oxford University and has translated more than fifty books from the Bulgarian, Catalan, Galician and Spanish languages for New Directions, Penguin Random House, Shearsman Books and others. He has written three books about the English language, the latest of which is *Stones Of Ithaca* (2019) about meaning inside words and the language of the environment. He is currently studying for a Certificate in Orthodox Christian Studies in Cambridge and serves as a subdeacon in the Bulgarian Orthodox Church. He directs the publishing house Small Stations Press. His personal website is www.stonesofithaca.com.